SHAPING THE DEBATE

Defining and Discussing
FREE SPEECH

Christy Mihaly

Rourke
Educational Media

A Division of
Carson
Dellosa
Education

rourkeeducationalmedia.com

W9-BXO-055

Before Reading: *Building Background Knowledge and Vocabulary*

Building background knowledge can help children process new information and build upon what they already know. Before reading a book, it is important to tap into what children already know about the topic. This will help them develop their vocabulary and increase their reading comprehension.

Questions and Activities to Build Background Knowledge:

1. Look at the front cover of the book and read the title. What do you think this book will be about?
2. What do you already know about this topic?
3. Take a book walk and skim the pages. Look at the table of contents, photographs, captions, and bold words. Did these text features give you any information or predictions about what you will read in this book?

Vocabulary: *Vocabulary Is Key to Reading Comprehension*

Use the following directions to prompt a conversation about each word.

- Read the vocabulary words.
- What comes to mind when you see each word?
- What do you think each word means?

Vocabulary Words:
- *absolute*
- *aspect*
- *authoritarian*
- *censors*
- *commemorate*
- *Communist*
- *discrimination*
- *dissent*
- *internment*
- *pardoned*
- *penalize*
- *substantially*

During Reading: *Reading for Meaning and Understanding*

To achieve deep comprehension of a book, children are encouraged to use close reading strategies. During reading, it is important to have children stop and make connections. These connections result in deeper analysis and understanding of a book.

Close Reading a Text

During reading, have children stop and talk about the following:

- Any confusing parts
- Any unknown words
- Text to text, text to self, text to world connections
- The main idea in each chapter or heading

Encourage children to use context clues to determine the meaning of any unknown words. These strategies will help children learn to analyze the text more thoroughly as they read.

When you are finished reading this book, turn to page 46 for **Text-Dependent Questions** and an **Extension Activity**.

TABLE OF CONTENTS

CHAPTER ONE

FREE SPEECH AND THE FLAG

Americans are free to speak their minds. In the United States, freedom of speech means that people can express their opinions in person, in writing, on TV, on the internet, and everywhere. They can even express opinions that are unpopular or that are critical of government leaders.

The American flag is a familiar symbol of the country. Burning it is a powerful expression of political **dissent**. People who protested the Vietnam War in the 1960s burned the flag. Flag burning was used by students at American University in 2016 as a way to protest the results of the recent presidential election.

After the November 2016 election, many people exercised their freedom of speech with colorful messages on this subway wall.

Some people think that burning the flag should be illegal. But the First Amendment to the U.S. Constitution gives people the right to protest. That includes the right to engage in actions that some consider unpatriotic. The student protesters were saying they thought their country was in serious trouble. They were exercising their freedom of speech.

When people engage in peaceful protest, they're exercising their freedom of speech and freedom of assembly.

The First Amendment

"Congress shall make no law respecting an establishment of religion, or prohibiting the free exercise thereof; or abridging the freedom of speech, or of the press; or the right of the people peaceably to assemble, and to petition the government for a redress of grievances."

Free speech is a building block of democracy. Americans treasure this right—even when they find others' opinions deeply offensive. Actor-activist George Takei defended protesters' right to burn the flag. As a child during World War II, California-born Takei was imprisoned in a U.S. detention camp for Japanese-Americans. He stated, "I pledged allegiance to the flag every morning inside an **internment** camp. I would never burn one, but I'd die to protect the right to do so."

In the 1960s, George Takei starred as Lieutenant Sulu on the TV series *Star Trek*. He was one of the few Asian-American actors appearing regularly on television at that time.

Between 1942 and 1945, more than 100,000 people of Japanese ancestry were held in isolated internment camps like Tule Lake, in California, pictured here. Although the majority of those interned were United States citizens, some Americans argued that Japanese Americans would be loyal to Japan in World War II, rather than to the United States.

The United States Constitution, which was written in 1787 and went into effect in 1789, is the oldest written national constitution still in use by a modern nation.

What Is Speech?

The Constitution protects free expression, including spoken words, words on paper, online posts, movies, television, theater, dance, art, video games, political signs, messages on clothing, symbols, gestures, and political donations. It also protects the right NOT to speak—for example, to remain silent during the pledge to the flag.

CHAPTER TWO

FREE SPEECH MILESTONES

The U.S. Constitution, written in 1787, created a strong federal government. However, some American leaders worried this government had too much power. They wanted to guarantee the rights of individuals. So, in 1791, the first ten amendments to the Constitution—known as the Bill of Rights—were added.

"Scene at the Signing of the Constitution of the United States" was painted by Howard Chandler Christy in 1940. The painting, which hangs on the wall at the United States Capitol, shows George Washington presiding on the right, with Benjamin Franklin and Alexander Hamilton in the center foreground.

Congress of the United States

begun and held at the City of New York, on

Wednesday the fourth of March, one thousand seven hundred and eighty nine.

In 1789, Congress approved 12 constitutional amendments. The states later ratified ten of these, which became effective as the Bill of Rights in 1791.

The Bill of Rights

Beyond the First Amendment, the Bill of Rights guarantees freedoms including: The right to bear arms (Second Amendment); protection from unreasonable search and seizure (Fourth); right not to incriminate oneself (Fifth); right to a speedy trial (Sixth); trial by jury (Seventh); and protection from cruel and unusual punishment (Eighth).

Although the First Amendment clearly guaranteed freedom of speech, Americans weren't yet sure what "free speech" included. In England, sedition—encouraging opposition to the king—was prohibited. Some thought the U.S. should follow the same rule.

James Madison

James Madison
1751–1836

James Madison drafted the plan for a strong United States central government, which was incorporated into the Constitution in 1787. He believed the original Constitution protected individual rights by limiting the government's powers. However, Madison later wrote and advocated for the addition of the Bill of Rights.

John Adams was the second president of the United States, during a time when war between Great Britain and France caused political unrest. His signature on the Alien and Sedition Acts is widely believed to have led to his defeat after a single term in office.

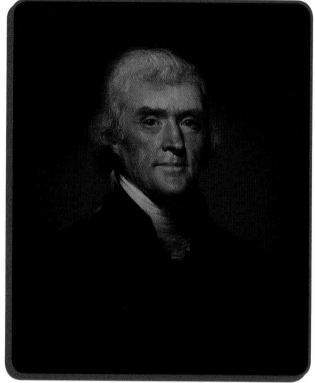

Thomas Jefferson, the drafter of the Declaration of Independence and third president of the United States, believed in a limited role for the national government.

In 1798, supporters of President John Adams pushed a new law through Congress. The Sedition Act made it a crime to insult the president. The government started jailing critics of Adams. Adams's opponents—led by Thomas Jefferson—argued this suppression of opinions violated the First Amendment. Outrage over the Sedition Act contributed to Adams's loss to Jefferson in the 1800 election. As the new president, Jefferson **pardoned** everyone convicted under the Sedition Act. Americans, he said, had the right to criticize their leaders.

FIFTH CONGRESS OF THE UNITED STATES:

At the Second Session.

Begun and held at the city of *Philadelphia*, in the state of PENNSYLVANIA, on *Monday*, the thirteenth of *November*, one thousand seven hundred and ninety-seven.

An ACT *in addition to the act, entitled "An Act for the punishment of certain crimes against the United States."*

BE it enacted by the Senate and House of Representatives of the United States of America, in Congress assembled. That if any person shall unlawfully combine or conspire together, with intent to oppose any measure or measures of the government of the United States, which are or shall be directed by proper authority, or to impede the operation of any law of the United States, or to intimidate or prevent any person, holding a place or office in or under the government of the United States, from undertaking, performing or executing his trust or duty; and if any person or persons, with intent as aforesaid, shall counsel, advise or attempt to procure any insurrection, riot, unlawful assembly, or combination, whether such conspiracy, threatening, counsel, advice, or attempt shall have the proposed effect or not, he or they shall be deemed guilty of a high misdemeanor, and on conviction, before any court of the United States having jurisdiction thereof, shall be punished by a fine not exceeding five thousand dollars, and by imprisonment during a term not less than six months nor exceeding five years; and further, at the discretion of the court may be holden to find sureties for his good behaviour in such sum, and for such time, as the said court may direct.

Sect. 2. And be it further enacted, That if any person shall write, print, utter or publish, or shall cause or procure to be written, printed, uttered or published, or shall knowingly and willingly assist or aid in writing, printing, uttering or publishing any false, scandalous and malicious writing or writings against the government of the United States, or either House of the Congress of the United States, or the President of the United States, with intent to defame the said government, or either House of the said Congress, or the said President, or to bring them, or either of them, into contempt or disrepute; or to excite against them, or either of them, the hatred of the good people of the United States; or to stir up sedition within the United States, or to excite any unlawful combinations therein, for opposing or resisting any law of the United States, or any act of the President of the United States, done in pursuance of any such law, or of the powers in him vested by the Constitution of the United States; or to resist, oppose, or defeat any such law or act; or to aid, encourage or abet any hostile designs of any foreign nation against the United States, their people or government, then such person, being thereof convicted before any court of the United States having jurisdiction thereof, shall be punished by

Sect. 3.

Matthew Lyon: Free Speech Hero

Congressman Matthew Lyon of Vermont disliked John Adams. Lyon not only disagreed with Adams's politics, he called the President ridiculous, greedy, power-hungry, and pompous. Lyon was convicted and imprisoned under the Sedition Act. But Vermont voters rallied to his cause. Lyon ran for re-election from his jail cell, and won.

Approved July 14, 1798.
John Adams

I certify that this Act did originate in the Senate.

In the 1950s, the United States experienced a different First Amendment crisis. The nation was engaged in a "Cold War" against the Soviet Union and its ruling **Communist** Party. The U.S. and Soviet governments were locked in competition to expand their power and influence around the globe. Americans feared there were Soviet spies everywhere. They suspected that members of the Communist Party in the U.S. were disloyal to America. Playing on these fears, Senator Joseph McCarthy began Senate hearings in 1950 to find anyone with "communist sympathies."

Langston Hughes Testifies

Langston Hughes, African-American poet and advocate for equal rights, was one of many important literary figures called before McCarthy's committee. The committee asked about his previously stated support of communist ideas. His testimony stated in part:

"My interest in whatever may be considered political has been non-theoretical, non-sectarian, and largely really emotional and born out of my own need to find some kind of way of thinking about this whole problem of myself, segregated, poor, colored, and how I can adjust to this whole problem of helping to build America when sometimes I can not even get into a school or a lecture or a concert or in the South go the library and get a book out."

The influence of Senator McCarthy (pictured here) declined after Senate hearings investigating supposed communists in the U.S. military were televised. The Army's lawyer scolded McCarthy, "Have you no sense of decency?"

Margaret Chase Smith, a Republican from Maine, was the first woman to serve in both the House of Representatives and the Senate. In delivering her June 1950 "Declaration of Conscience" to the Senate, she became the first senator to stand up against the scare tactics of fellow Republican Senator Joseph McCarthy.

McCarthy summoned thousands of innocent people before his committee, accusing them of disloyalty. He destroyed many reputations and lives—without any real evidence. Amid the hysteria, anyone resisting McCarthy or defending communists was called "un-American." As Senator Margaret Chase Smith pointed out, McCarthy was trampling fundamental American principles: "the right to criticize; the right to hold unpopular beliefs; the right to protest; the right of independent thought." Public opinion finally turned against McCarthy. In 1954, the Senate ended the hearings.

CHAPTER THREE

NOT ALL SPEECH IS FREE

The First Amendment doesn't confer an **absolute** right to say anything. Significantly, it prohibits only *government* actions that hinder free speech. It doesn't prevent private parties from controlling others' expression. For example, employers can tell employees what to say and not say.

Colin Kaepernick's Anthem Protest

During the 2016 NFL (National Football League) season, San Francisco 49ers quarterback Colin Kaepernick started kneeling during the pre-game national anthem to protest police shootings of black Americans. Others joined to protest racial injustice. Some people—including team owners—said players should stand to show respect. As private companies, teams could punish players for kneeling.

In 2017, Colin Kaepernick filed a claim against the NFL alleging the league had colluded to prevent him from signing a contract to play with any team after his 2016 protests. He reached a settlement with the NFL in February 2019.

17

Not all types of speech are protected equally. The Constitution gives greatest protection to political speech, or communications about issues and candidates. That's because when people can criticize elected officials and discuss competing viewpoints, they better understand what their government is doing and become better-informed voters.

Candidates in the 2016 presidential campaign exercised their free speech rights both to discuss political issues and to make personal attacks against one another.

Alexander Meiklejohn, pictured here on the cover of *Time* magazine in 1928, pointed out that freedom of speech was important in enabling voters to make informed decisions.

A Marketplace of Ideas

Political theorist Alexander Meiklejohn criticized the McCarthy hearings and defended the rights of communists to teach. In 1948 he wrote, "The principle of the freedom of speech springs from the necessities of the program of self-government. ... To be afraid of ideas, any idea, is to be unfit for self-government."

Police may arrest protesters if they cause injuries, damage property, or violate other laws.

Speech that is not about politics is less protected. Governments can **penalize** communications such as pornography and obscenity, or defamation—false statements that harm someone's reputation. Laws can require advertisements to be accurate. And there is no constitutional right to plagiarize, or use another's work without permission.

Finally, even political speech can be regulated. Governments may stop speech that intentionally provokes immediate violence. They can also specify the time, place, or manner of protests. For example, cities may require permits for demonstrations and restrict the hours, noise levels, or locations of protests. But regulations that entirely prevent people from communicating their political messages are unconstitutional.

CHAPTER FOUR

SCHOOLS, STUDENTS, AND SPEECH

School rules may restrict what students are allowed to say. However, students do have free speech rights. As the U.S. Supreme Court said, students don't "shed their constitutional rights to freedom of speech or expression at the schoolhouse gate."

The leading case is *Tinker v. Des Moines*. In 1965, 13-year-old Mary Beth Tinker and several fellow students wore black armbands (with peace signs) to school to protest the Vietnam War. Their school suspended them. The Supreme Court found this violated the First Amendment. The justices explained that when students express political views, schools can punish them only for conduct that **substantially** disrupts the school's functioning. Wearing armbands, they concluded, wasn't sufficiently disruptive.

Mary Beth Tinker, her brother John Tinker, and several other students were suspended from school for wearing armbands like this.

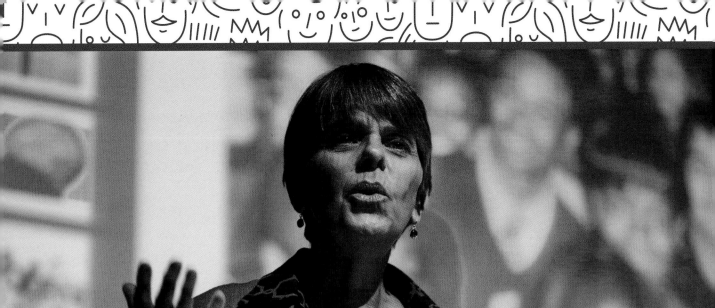

Mary Beth Tinker

Mary Beth Tinker's armband started a four-year legal battle over free speech. Mary Beth, her brother, and a friend went to court but lost in the federal trial court and appeal court. The Supreme Court eventually upheld their right to protest.

In 2013, Mary Beth Tinker, shown here, quit her job as a nurse to focus on speaking about the First Amendment. She tells young people "they can be a

The *Tinker* case involved a public school. Private schools, not covered by the First Amendment, could legally prohibit students from speaking freely. Many nonetheless support their students' self-expression.

Public schools can enforce rules against obscene speech or remarks encouraging violence or illegal activity. In one case, the Supreme Court said a school could suspend a student for displaying a "Bong Hits 4 Jesus" banner because it encouraged illegal drug use.

Regularly enforced school rules, such as attendance requirements, can also interfere with free expression. In 2018, after the mass shooting at Marjory Stoneman Douglas High School, thousands of students joined demonstrations calling for gun control. Many participated in the National School Walkout to **commemorate** the 17 victims. Some schools supported these activities. Others warned that students would be punished for missing classes. Such punishment would not violate the First Amendment if schools simply applied normal attendance policies.

These California students joined the National School Walkout to protest gun violence and call for controls on firearms.

What About Dress Codes?

Schools can prohibit clothing that distracts from learning, such as vulgar or gang-related attire. They can also limit clothes with political messages, but only with content-neutral rules. A school could ban all hats, for example, but it couldn't prohibit "Gay Rights" and "Greenpeace" hats while allowing "NRA" and "Pro-Life" hats.

CHAPTER FIVE

SPEECH AROUND THE WORLD

Authoritarian governments seek to control information and eliminate dissenting voices. In China, for example, the government monitors internet use and forbids online research about certain topics. China blocks thousands of websites and apps, including Facebook, YouTube, Twitter, and Google. Many other countries also restrict internet use, among them Saudi Arabia, Iran, and North Korea.

China's ruling Communist Party monitors internet use and blocks web content that it considers contrary to the government's interests.

CHINA

Winnie the Pooh: Not Welcome in China

In 2017, Chinese government *censors* blocked social media sites from using images of the Walt Disney character Winnie the Pooh. Memes in China had used the cartoon bear to represent—and make fun of—Chinese President Xi Jinping.

Book burning has been used in many times and places as a demonstration of censorship. Public bonfires are built to destroy books and other materials that are considered improper for cultural, religious, or political reasons.

Many countries censor books, music, and art. India, for example, has banned books that portray the Hindu or Muslim religions unfavorably. Governments in China, Turkey, Uganda, and elsewhere have shut down art exhibits and films, banned songs, and fined and imprisoned artists because officials disapproved of their art or their messages.

In 2018, Cuba announced new rules prohibiting artists or performers from presenting or selling their work without government permission. Artists protesting the requirements were arrested. The government said it wanted to maintain high standards of quality in Cuban art. But the requirement of governmental approval limits artists' freedom of expression.

In 2018, Abdel Fattah al-Sisi was elected to a second term as Egypt's president, receiving 97% of the vote. His political opponents had been jailed, deported, or otherwise prevented from running against him.

In some countries, speaking out requires great courage, and those who publicly disagree with authorities may "disappear." In Egypt, the government of Abdel Fattah al-Sisi declared the political party of his opponents (the Muslim Brotherhood) a terrorist group. Since 2013, Egypt has killed or imprisoned hundreds of Muslim Brotherhood members and others who criticized government policies. Many are held in undisclosed locations.

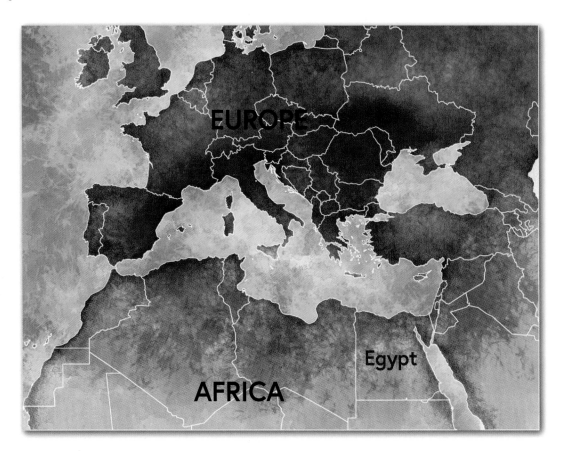

EUROPE

AFRICA

Egypt

Pussy Riot is a Russian band of artists and political activists who have staged many protest actions. Group members often wear colorful balaclavas—head and face coverings—during protests and performances.

Pussy Riot: Creative Protest

At soccer's 2018 World Cup final in Russia, members of Russian punk band Pussy Riot brought worldwide attention to their demands. They stormed the field, calling for Russia to release political prisoners. In 2012, two band members were imprisoned for nearly two years for performing a protest criticizing Russian President Vladimir Putin.

Maria Alyokhina was imprisoned almost two years for her part in Pussy Riot's 2012 "punk prayer" performance. Since her release she has campaigned for prisoners' rights and other causes.

Nadezhda Tolokonnikova was the second Pussy Riot member who spent nearly two years in prison after the group's anti-Putin protest in a church. She also continued her activism after her release.

Democratic countries may also restrict the expression of certain opinions. In Germany, after World War II, the new government took aggressive actions to prevent a future Nazi regime. It banned the display of Nazi symbols. In Germany, it is illegal to engage in racist speech or to deny that the Holocaust occurred.

In 1945, after the Allies defeated Germany in World War II, they banned the display of Nazi symbols, including flags, statues, and monuments. Later, they convened the Nuremberg Trials, where German military leaders were brought to justice for their war crimes.

CHAPTER SIX

U.S. FREE SPEECH CONTROVERSIES

Many countries restrict hate speech—words attacking people of certain races, religions, and other groups. In the United States, however, the First Amendment protects all expression, even hate speech—unless it involves a direct threat or causes immediate violence.

This **aspect** of freedom of speech can be difficult to accept. In August 2017, neo-Nazis and white nationalists—white people advocating a white national identity—held a Unite the Right rally in Charlottesville, Virginia.

They marched with torches, shouting Nazi slogans. Charlottesville's Mayor Michael Signer called it a "cowardly parade of hatred, bigotry, racism, and intolerance." Later, one white nationalist drove into a crowd of counter-protesters, killing a woman and causing many injuries.

Police blocked a Charlottesville street on August 12, 2017, after a driver drove his car into the crowd of people opposing the white nationalist demonstration. Heather Heyer was killed, and

Crowds rallied against the white supremacists in Charlottesville, Virginia.

The First Amendment does not protect such violence. The Charlottesville driver was tried and convicted of murder. But the First Amendment gives all voices the right to be heard. The government can't stop a demonstration based on the unpopularity of speakers' opinions or the possibility of counter-protests. Rather, officials are expected to work with police to assure the safety of protesters and the public.

Campus Controversy

At the Charlottesville rally, University of Nevada, Reno (UNR) student Peter Cvjetanovic was photographed yelling white nationalist chants. Thousands petitioned for UNR to expel him. University officials declined. They explained that while they rejected racism and bigotry, Cvjetanovic had a right to express his views and remain a student.

College students on some campuses have sought to bar white nationalist speakers. But public universities can't exclude speakers based on their views. Such institutions, while fighting **discrimination** and harassment, must also protect free speech.

The controversial personality Milo Yiannopoulos was banned from Twitter for his harassment and abuse of others. His statements have been called racist, misogynist, and homophobic, and his public appearances have been met with protests.

Crowds protested a 2017 speech by Milo Yiannopoulos at the University of California, Berkeley.

Increasingly, people discuss political issues on social media. Social media companies are private, so they can prohibit offensive content. These companies have been criticized for allowing false and hateful posts. Some posts have led users to commit hate crimes. The debate continues over how much censorship these companies should exercise.

Unconstitutional Blocking?

President Trump communicated frequently through his personal @realDonaldTrump Twitter account after becoming president. Often, followers disagreed with Trump's tweets. Sometimes, Trump blocked people from his account. Was that legal? In May 2018, a court said no. Preventing people from viewing or discussing the President's posts, it said, interfered with their freedom of speech. Trump appealed.

Donald J. Trump ✓
@realDonaldTrump
45th President of the United States of America
📍 Washington, DC

45 FOLLOWING   32,1M FOLLOWERS

TWEETS   TWEETS & REPLIES   MEDIA   LIKES

Donald J. Trump ✓ @realDonaldTru...
2 million more people just dropped out of ObamaCare. It is in a death spiral. Obstructionist Democrats gave up, have no answer = resist!

↩ 10,2K   ⇄ 7.125   ♥ 26K

Donald J. Trump ✓ @realDon...
Heading to the Great St... to talk about JOBS progress bei... reportin...

Corporations also have a right to political speech under the First Amendment. They can buy advertisements supporting or opposing political candidates. The Supreme Court, in the *Citizens United v. FEC* case, allowed corporations to spend unlimited amounts on political advertising. Some critics believe this ruling gave wealthy corporations too much influence on elections.

The Federal Election Commission

The Federal Election Commission (FEC) is an independent regulatory agency whose purpose is to enforce campaign finance law in United States federal elections.

Despite such controversies, international polling indicates that Americans value free speech more highly than people in other countries do. Some might prefer to silence certain opinions. Others, however, contend that open debate is best, and that the First Amendment requires nothing less.

On the wall of the Cox Corridor in the United States Capitol, this statement by Benjamin Franklin is displayed: "Without Freedom of Thought, there can be no such Thing as Wisdom; and no such Thing as publick Liberty, without Freedom of Speech."

PRACTICE PREPARING FOR A DEBATE

People explain issues and solve problems through discussion. Debates are formal discussions about an issue. Debate participants present facts they have gathered from reliable sources. They present this information as they try to convince listeners that their opinions about an issue are correct.

Supplies

- paper
- pencil
- books on your topic and/or internet access

Directions:

1. Decide the topic you will research.

2. Write a question that will shape your debate. Example: Should religion be taught in public schools?

3. Write your proposition or opposition statement. Proposition example: Religion should be taught in public schools. Opposition example: Religion should not be taught in public schools.

4. Research your topic using a variety of sources. Make a list of the facts you find and note the source of each fact next to it.

5. Practice presenting your argument.

6. Flip the script! Follow steps 1–5 again, this time preparing with facts that support the other side.

Bonus: Form a debate club with your friends. Assign a new topic regularly. Give each person equal time to present their arguments.